Original title:
The Dream Ship's Voyage

Author: Jaxon Kingsley
ISBN HARDBACK: 978-9916-90-764-1
ISBN PAPERBACK: 978-9916-90-765-8

Journeying on Night's Gentle Wave

Beneath the stars, we sail so free,
Whispers of night, our melody.
The moonlight guides our silent quest,
In dreams we find our hearts at rest.

With every wave, a tale unfolds,
Of treasures lost and journeys bold.
The night embraces all we seek,
In shadows deep, our spirits speak.

The Harbor of Illusions

In stillness lies a distant shore,
Where echoes of our hopes restore.
Fleeting moments, like whispered breeze,
In this harbor, time seems to freeze.

Reflections dance on water's face,
Caught in dreams, we find our place.
With every tide, a secret flows,
The heart's safe haven, nobody knows.

Tides of Memory and Wonder

Waves of memory crash and play,
Reminding us of yesterday.
Each crest and trough, a story told,
Of laughter shared and friendships bold.

In the twilight, secrets weave,
Golden threads we dare believe.
Carried by the tide's embrace,
We journey on through time and space.

Echoes of Hidden Shores

Where the land meets the restless sea,
Lies a place where we roam free.
Hidden shores call out our name,
In quiet whispers, igniting flame.

Through tangled paths and shifting sand,
We walk together, hand in hand.
The echoes of our laughter ring,
In every heart, a new song to sing.

Charting the Stars of Reverie

In twilight's hue, dreams take flight,
Mapping the heavens, a guiding light.
With whispers soft, they dance and soar,
A cosmic dance, forevermore.

Promises inked in the night sky,
Each star a wish, a silent sigh.
Navigating paths where dreams abide,
In the heart's embrace, we confide.

Waves of Yesterday’s Whispers

Echoes linger, soft like the tide,
Memories murmur, nowhere to hide.
Each wave that crashes, tales of the past,
In the sea of time, forever cast.

Seagulls call, as shadows fall,
Whispers of journeys, they enthrall.
Carried away on a breeze so fine,
Yesterday's secrets forever entwined.

Floating Beyond the Realm of Tomorrow

Drifting softly on dreams so bright,
Beyond the grasp of morning light.
Time unravels, a gentle stream,
We float together, lost in a dream.

Horizons beckon, far and near,
Whispers of hope, cradled in fear.
Beyond the dawn, where time stands still,
Floating onward, we chase our will.

Embarking on the Veil's Silken Cruise

Set sail on whispers, soft and light,
Through veils of silk, into the night.
Each moment glimmers, a treasure rare,
Embarking on dreams, a journey to share.

The winds of fate guide our course,
As stars alight with gentle force.
With hearts unbound, we sail away,
To horizons new, where hopes will sway.

The Harbor of Dreams and Delights

In the quiet morn, dreams awake,
Whispers of wishes, softly they make.
Colors of twilight spill on the sea,
Guiding lost souls where they long to be.

Laughter and joy echo from the shore,
Memories painted, forever to store.
Sails of adventure await the bold,
In this harbor, wonders unfold.

Stars twinkle gently, a lantern's gleam,
Filling the night with a shimmer of dream.
Here, every heart finds a place to belong,
In the harbor of dreams, where spirits grow strong.

Legends of the Soaring Night

Under the moon, legends take flight,
Stories of heroes written in light.
Winds carry tales from days of yore,
Whispering secrets long lost on the shore.

Owls sing softly, their voices a guide,
Through the dark woods, where shadows reside.
Echoes of past weave through the trees,
Unfolding the mysteries that float on the breeze.

Constellations watch over, silent and wise,
Mapping the paths of the wandering skies.
Each star a promise, a memory bright,
In the embrace of the legendary night.

A Drifting Heart on Cosmic Waves

Floating through galaxies, far and wide,
A heart adrift on the celestial tide.
Stars like beacons, they dance and they play,
Guiding a soul in the cosmic ballet.

Nebulas swirl in a colorful haze,
Painting the darkness in vibrant displays.
Gravity pulls and it tugs at the dreams,
As the universe hums its soft, soothing themes.

Through stardust pathways, I wander alone,
Seeking the whispers of worlds yet unknown.
Each comet's trail a story untold,
In this vast expanse, my heart grows bold.

Searching for Shores of Memory

In the twilight haze, memories flow,
Waves whisper tales from long ago.
Footprints in sand, where time leaves its trace,
Searching for shores, a familiar place.

Seagulls above, in their graceful flight,
Calling to hearts lost in the night.
Echoes of laughter, they linger and play,
On the shores of memory, where dreams sway.

The tide brings moments, both bitter and sweet,
A symphony playing beneath my feet.
Each wave a reminder of love's gentle art,
Searching for shores that reside in my heart.

Cartographer of the Astral Sea

Amidst the stars, I chart my course,
Mapping dreams, a gentle force.
Constellations guide my weary hands,
In the void, where silence stands.

With ink of light, I trace the skies,
Unraveling truths, as darkness flies.
Galaxies weave their tales so grand,
In the depths, I understand.

Nebulas bloom, a cosmic dance,
Each twinkle holds a fleeting chance.
Through asteroids, I glide like mist,
Where wishes fade, I still persist.

Eternal night my canvas wide,
Guided by the starlit tide.
In the map of souls, I find my way,
A cartographer, night and day.

Windswept Dreams and Distant Shores

On windswept dunes, the dreams take flight,
Chasing echoes into the night.
Distant shores call with stories untold,
Where the heart dares to be bold.

Seagulls cry, their wings embrace,
Salt-kissed air, a sweet embrace.
Each grain of sand, a memory spun,
In the horizon, life has begun.

The waves dance softly, secrets to share,
Carrying whispers through the air.
Moonlit paths lead over the deep,
Guarding treasures that the ocean keeps.

With every tide, new hopes arise,
Beneath the vast, open skies.
Windswept dreams guide the way ahead,
To shores where all fears have fled.

Horizons that Whisper in the Night

Beneath the veil of stars, they speak,
Horizons stretch, mysterious and meek.
Silent secrets in the twilight glow,
Where shadows linger, and hopes bestow.

Each whisper holds a tale profound,
In the stillness, lost souls are found.
Dreams entwine like threads of fate,
In the darkness, they patiently wait.

The moonlight casts a gentle smile,
Guiding hearts to wander awhile.
With every gust, the night confides,
In whispered breezes, the spirit glides.

Embrace the dawn with open heart,
For in the night, we find our part.
Horizons expand with every breath,
In this twilight, we dance with death.

Tides of Belief and Serenity

In whispers soft, the tides arise,
They carry hopes and silent sighs.
Each wave that crashes, dreams set free,
A dance of faith, for you and me.

Beneath the moon's embrace tonight,
The stars align, a guiding light.
With every ebb, the heart finds peace,
In quiet moments, doubts release.

The shores may shift, but we remain,
Anchored strong through joy and pain.
In sunlit dawns or stormy nights,
Our spirits soar on boundless heights.

So trust the tides, their gentle flow,
Through valleys deep, and peaks of snow.
For in belief, we find our way,
Serenity blooms, come what may.

Sailing through Enchanted Mists

In misty realms where dreams take flight,
We sail through shadows, chasing light.
The whispers call from depths unknown,
A voyage crafted, all our own.

With every stroke, the fog unveils,
Secrets wrapped in ancient tales.
The waves, they dance with magic's grace,
As wonder paints each hidden place.

The winds of fate, they guide us true,
Through enchanting whispers, skies of blue.
In every breath, the journey swells,
As time dissolves in ocean's spells.

Together we find what hearts can dream,
In every heartbeat, a silken seam.
Through enchanted mists, our spirits soar,
The voyage calls, forevermore.

Ethereal Pathways of the Mind

Through corridors of thought we roam,
In silent reveries, we find home.
Each step, a thread, a story spun,
In ethereal realms where time is none.

The echoes whisper, secrets bare,
A tapestry woven with dreams that dare.
In shifting shadows, wisdom flows,
As the mind unravels, the spirit grows.

Illuminated paths weave bright,
Guiding the lost towards the light.
In every moment, a choice to make,
A bridge of thought, a dawn to break.

So wander freely, let thoughts entwine,
In the labyrinth vast, where stars align.
For in the depths of the mind's embrace,
We find our truth, our sacred space.

Odysseys Beyond the Flesh

Beyond the skin, the spirit flies,
To realms where earthly tether dies.
In odysseys of heart and soul,
We seek the essence, to be whole.

With every breath, the journey starts,
Exploring vast and sacred arts.
In cosmic dances, we shall meet,
Where love transcends, and souls compete.

Through galaxies, our hearts ignite,
In sacred spaces, purest light.
A tapestry of lives entwined,
In unity, we're beautifully blind.

So take the leap beyond the skin,
Embrace the vastness found within.
For odysseys await the brave,
In realms where only spirits wave.

Sailing on Celestial Winds

Beneath the stars we glide so free,
On silver waves of mystery.
The whispers of the night we seek,
With every breath, our spirits speak.

Through cosmic tides, our hearts expand,
In rhythmic dance, we take a stand.
Charting paths where dreams can soar,
Unfurling sails forevermore.

The moonlight guides our way ahead,
In tranquil silence, visions spread.
The universe, a canvas wide,
As we embrace the cosmic tide.

With each horizon that we chase,
We find our truth in boundless space.
Together, sailing hand in hand,
On celestial winds, we take our stand.

The Twilight Flotilla of Imagination

In twilight's glow, we set our course,
On boats of dreams, we find our force.
With sails of hope, we navigate,
Through colored skies, we celebrate.

Worlds of wonder flicker bright,
As shadows dance in fading light.
Each wave a story yet untold,
In whispers soft, our dreams unfold.

Through gentle breezes, softly led,
We sail the realms where visions tread.
A flotilla of thoughts and schemes,
In twilight's grasp, we weave our dreams.

Let hearts be light, let worries cease,
In this embrace, we find our peace.
Together, bound, we float and sway,
On twilight's edge, we drift away.

The Voyage of Whimsical Souls

Set forth we did, with laughter bright,
On winds that sang of pure delight.
Each wave a spark of joy and grace,
In whimsical dreams, we found our place.

The ocean’s brush, a painter's hand,
Invites us to a vibrant land.
With every stroke, a story’s spun,
Where whimsical souls unite as one.

Through tempest’s roar and calm’s embrace,
We sail the seas, lost in the chase.
For every sigh and joyful leap,
Our hearts are secrets the oceans keep.

In laughter’s echo, find your tune,
Beneath the watchful gaze of moon.
Together bound, our spirits free,
We voyage on, by destiny.

Chasing Distant Dreamscapes

Across the seas of time and space,
We chase the dreams that leave a trace.
With every wave, a wish in flight,
To distant shores, we seek the light.

The stars above, our guiding flame,
In whispered winds, we call their name.
On shores unknown, our hearts align,
In dreamscapes vast, our souls entwine.

Each horizon beckons with delight,
As dawn breaks forth, igniting night.
Through vivid landscapes, we will roam,
In every heart, we find a home.

So sail with courage, hearts ablaze,
For dreamers chase through endless days.
Together we will cross each tide,
In distant dreamscapes, side by side.

Whispers of the Celestial Sea

In the night sky, stars softly gleam,
Waves of cosmic light, a tranquil dream.
Celestial whispers, secrets untold,
Guiding lost souls, brave and bold.

Under the moon's gentle embrace,
Time slows down in this sacred space.
Whispers of love, echo and glide,
In the celestial sea, our hearts confide.

Galaxies dance with a luminous grace,
Each star a beacon in infinite space.
Embracing the night, we soar and we weave,
In the whispers of dreams, we truly believe.

Sailors of Stardust

We are the sailors of stardust bright,
Navigating realms of shimmering light.
With hearts as our compass, we set our course,
Through cosmic oceans, we feel the force.

Drifting on currents of nebula's hue,
Charting the paths where dreams come true.
With sails made of hope, we journey afar,
Guided by the glow of the evening star.

Whispers of galaxies call us near,
In the embrace of the universe, we hear.
Together we sail, unafraid of the test,
In the arms of stardust, we find our rest.

Navigating Night's Embrace

In the deep of night, shadows entwine,
We navigate passages where stars align.
The moon casts its glow, a silver guide,
Leading us gently where mysteries hide.

Through whispers of darkness, our spirits soar,
With every heartbeat, we long for more.
Embracing the silence, we dance with fate,
In night's warm embrace, we patiently wait.

Stars flicker softly, a celestial song,
In the tapestry of time, we belong.
Navigating night, hand in hand we roam,
In the heart of the cosmos, we find our home.

Journey to the Realm of Reveries

Come take my hand, let's drift away,
To the realm of reveries where dreams play.
With each step forward, the world fades away,
In landscapes of wonder, we long to stay.

Colors so vibrant, like a painter's brush,
In the realm of reveries, our hearts rush.
Floating on clouds, where wishes ignite,
In this dreamscape of magic, we bask in delight.

Where time is a treasure, and laughter is free,
We dance on the edges of what we can't see.
Journey with me to all we dreamt of,
In the realm of reveries, we rise above.

Horizon of Hidden Hopes

Beyond the veil of dawn's soft light,
Whispers of dreams take flight.
Colors bloom in silent grace,
A world awaits to embrace.

In shadows dance the wishes fair,
Casting nets of love and care.
Mountains rise with stories old,
As hearts weave tales yet untold.

Each wave that laps the sandy shore,
Calls to spirits to explore.
With every sunrise, new roads appear,
Igniting courage, quelling fear.

So chase the horizon, run wild and free,
For it holds the future, just wait and see.
In the depths of dreams, may you find your way,
To the horizon where hopes forever stay.

Driftwood Dreams and Moonlit Maps

Carried by tides on celestial schemes,
Driftwood whispers of distant dreams.
Each knot a tale of journeys past,
Guiding the way to the stars amassed.

Beneath the moon's enchanting glow,
Moonlit maps in the waters flow.
Secrets hidden in silvery light,
Charting the course of the endless night.

Waves sing softly, a lullaby sweet,
Each rhythm a memory, each pulse a heartbeat.
With every glance at the sky's vast dome,
I find my way, no longer alone.

So follow the driftwood, let currents lead,
In dreams and moonlight, find what you need.
For in the heart of the untamed sea,
Lies the path to who you're meant to be.

Where Fantasies Set Sail

On ships of wonder, we rise and fall,
Through stormy nights and sunshine's call.
With sails unfurled, we brave the blue,
As fantasies beckon, guiding us through.

Each wave a whisper of tales untold,
In the cradle of time, we feel bold.
Sailing the seas of hope and desire,
Fires of passion endlessly inspire.

We chart the skies with dreams in sight,
Navigating shadows, chasing the light.
With every sunset, horizons unfold,
The magic of life in colors so bold.

So gather your courage, stow away fear,
For the horizon sings sweetly, 'Your time is near.'
In the arms of the ocean, embrace what you find,
For where fantasies sail, great joys unwind.

Echoes on the Ether Waves

In quiet echoes, voices rise,
Softly weaving through the skies.
On ether waves, a song takes flight,
Carrying dreams through the night.

Whispers of thoughts, both bright and rare,
Drifting gently through the air.
Each note a memory, a heartbeat's call,
In the silence, we find it all.

With every sigh, a feeling shared,
Across the vastness, hearts are bared.
Connection found where souls collide,
In the ether's arms, we confide.

So let the echoes guide your way,
For in their song, love's light may stay.
On the waves of sound, let go, be brave,
And find the treasures that silence gave.

The Enchanted Armada of Dreams

Sails unfurl upon the night,
Whispers soft, glowing bright.
Stars align, a guiding fleet,
Boundless journeys, hearts' retreat.

Waves of silver, gently sway,
Echoes of what dreams convey.
Each vessel holds a wish inside,
On moonlit tides, we now abide.

In the mist, familiar faces,
Hopeful hearts in secret places.
Through the realms of never-ending,
To the shores of dreams, ascending.

A voyage stitched with threads of light,
In every heart, a spark ignites.
Together through the azure mist,
The armada sails, we can't resist.

Ethereal Currents of Thought

Whispers float on streams of air,
Carried forth without a care.
Thoughts like ripples, quick to flow,
In the depths, our wonders grow.

Silent echoes, soft and clear,
Guiding minds, both far and near.
Dancing lightly on the breeze,
Crafting dreams with perfect ease.

Waves of meaning, ebb and swell,
In the heart, a secret spell.
Through the currents, truth does glide,
In the storm, we shall not hide.

Ethereal waves, a cosmic dance,
In each pulse, we find our chance.
Thoughts unite across the seas,
In their embrace, we feel at ease.

The Driftwood of Forgotten Dreams

Washed ashore, lost and alone,
Driftwood tells tales in soft tone.
Mementos of hopes, swept away,
Whispers of night, glimmers of day.

In the sand, we search for signs,
Echoes linger, intertwining lines.
Fragments of wishes, once so bright,
Now gather dust in fading light.

Each piece of wood, a tale concealed,\nUnraveled as the world is revealed.
Time's embrace holds them so dear,
Silent guardians of yesteryear.

Let us gather these lost remains,
Rekindle dreams through joy and pain.
With each heartbeat, we reclaim,
The driftwood's worth, we sign our name.

Passage Beyond the Sleepful Bay

Upon the dock, the twilight waits,
A gentle breeze, the hour's fates.
Boats at rest, in silent sway,
Whisper secrets of the bay.

Stars above, like dreams take flight,
Guiding souls into the night.
A passage formed of starlit beams,
Leading us to woven dreams.

Reflections dance on water's face,
Each ripple holds a hidden grace.
The calm embrace of night's perfume,
Cradles us in twilight's loom.

Beyond the bay, adventures call,
To distant shores, where wonders sprawl.
In the stillness, hearts shall soar,
As we embark to seek much more.

Canvas of the Midnight Tide

On waves that whisper secrets low,
The moon casts silver, soft aglow.
Stars twinkle like distant dreams,
In silence, the ocean softly screams.

Brushstrokes of night paint the sea,
A canvas of wild mystery.
Each ripple tells a tale untold,
As the tides embrace the dark and bold.

Gentle currents pull and sway,
In harmony, the nightbirds play.
With every splash, the heart can feel,
The magic of the ocean's reel.

Beneath the cloak of midnight's hue,
Adventures beckon, lost yet true.
The canvas waits with bated breath,
For strokes of courage beyond death.

Beyond the Veil of Dreams

In slumber's grasp, the world retreats,
Soft whispers weave, where nightlight beats.
A realm where shadows take their flight,
Beyond the veil of soft twilight.

Figures dance on silken streams,
Where reality bends to our dreams.
Each thought a feather, light and free,
In this ethereal tapestry.

Familiar faces, memories sway,
In color’s embrace, they gently play.
Woven destinies guide our way,
In dreamland's arms, we'll choose to stay.

With every dawn, a thread unspools,
Yet in our hearts, dreams stand as jewels.
Beyond the veil, they softly gleam,
A treasure chest of whispered dream.

The Odyssey of Unseen Shores

Beyond the horizon, whispers call,
To shores unseen, where shadows fall.
A journey vast, through time and space,
An odyssey in a silent place.

Waves crash softly on hidden sand,
Each step a promise, an unseen hand.
The compass spins in the twilight glow,
As currents guide where few dare go.

Islands of thought on the edge of mind,
In every echo, new worlds unwind.
Voices dance in the salty air,
Guiding the seeker through the dare.

With the wind as guide, the heart must roam,
In searching hearts, we find our home.
The unseen shores await our song,
Where the brave belong, where we belong.

Navigating the Cosmic Current

Stars like diamonds in endless space,
Flow through the heavens, a timeless race.
In cosmic currents, galaxies swirl,
Mysteries unfold, as dreams unfurl.

Celestial maps in starlit trails,
Guide our ships through radiant wails.
Each pulse of light, a whispered tune,
Drawing us closer to the moon.

Beyond the dark, the wonders wait,
In the arms of time, we'll navigate.
With every breath, a universe grows,
In this grand dance, the mystery flows.

So sail the skies on dreams' embrace,
Navigating through the vast, vast space.
In cosmic currents, our spirits soar,
Together, forever, to worlds explore.

Echoes of the Celestial Drift

In the silence where stars gleam bright,
Whispers of galaxies take flight.
Each twinkle tells a tale of old,
In cosmic arms, the night unfolds.

Nebulas dance, a vibrant swirl,
Painting the heavens, a radiant pearl.
Winds of time in orbits weave,
The secrets of the skies we believe.

A chorus sung by distant spheres,
Echoes of laughter, shadows of tears.
Through the void, the silence hums,
A lullaby of worlds yet to come.

Boundless realms in twilight's sigh,
Where dreams ascend and never die.
In stardust paths, our thoughts uplift,
Embracing all in celestial drift.

Sailing Through the Realm of Shadows

Beneath the veil of twilight's grace,
We sail the shadows, a hidden place.
With every wave that strokes the night,
We seek the glow of the lost light.

Whispers follow on ghostly trails,
Echoes of secrets through silent gales.
Guided by moonbeams, soft and pale,
We drift in dreams, on shadows' sails.

A dance with specters, ethereal and bold,
Stories entwined in the darkness told.
We wander realms where shadows bloom,
Awakening magic from the gloom.

In the stillness where heartbeats blend,
We find the paths where shadows send.
Adventures linger, alight with thrill,
As we sail through the shadows, time stands still.

A Sea of Starry Fantasies

Upon the waves of a starry sea,
Dreams unfurl like sails set free.
Each twinkle, a guide to distant lands,
Where fantasies bloom at our command.

With stardust sprinkled on evening's breath,
We chase the echoes of life and death.
From shores of wonder, we launch our quest,
In a realm where night and wishes rest.

Galaxies swirl in an endless dance,
In the hearts of dreamers who dare to glance.
A symphony played on the cosmic strings,
Where hope ignites and adventure sings.

The tide of dreams, relentless and grand,
Carries us forth to a promised land.
In this sea of fantasies, we roam free,
Bound by the laughter of eternity.

Twilight's Ethereal Expedition

In twilight's glow, the journey starts,
With whispered tales that warm our hearts.
Each step a brush on the canvas wide,
Where colors merge and shadows hide.

Stars awaken as the sun descends,
In the embrace where the day ends.
With every breath, a story we weave,
In the fabric of night, we dare to believe.

The horizon beckons with secrets untold,
Calling brave souls, daring and bold.
With courage stirring, we set our course,
Guided by dreams and an inner force.

Through valleys deep and mountains high,
We sail the twilight, our spirits fly.
In this expedition where wonders blend,
We find our hearts as the stars descend.

The Navigator's Lullaby

Rest your head, O sailor bold,
The stars will guide you through the cold.
With whispers soft, the waves will sing,
Of distant shores and future spring.

In dreams you'll find the compass true,
As gentle winds will carry you.
Fear not the shadows in the night,
For dawn will break with morning light.

With heart of oak, and eyes that gleam,
You'll sail beyond the silver stream.
Each twinkling star a beacon bright,
To lead you home by starry light.

So close your eyes, my daring friend,
Let lullabies of sailors blend.
With every tide, your spirit soar,
For the sea's embrace will keep you warm.

Mysteries of the Dreaming Ocean

Beneath the waves, stories untold,
Of ancient seas and mariners bold.
Whispers of fish, in currents fade,
Secrets of deep, where shadows wade.

In twilight's glow, the waters shift,
As moonlit beams in silence drift.
Each wave a tale, a mystery spun,
In the heart of the ocean, where dreams run.

Stars align in the vast expanse,
Drawn by the ocean's timeless dance.
Mysteries called by siren song,
In waters deep, where we belong.

With every tide, come wonders new,
A realm of magic, hidden from view.
In dreams we dive, beyond the foam,
To the ocean's depths, we find our home.

Fantasia on the Watery Horizon

Horizon glows with colors bright,
Where sky and sea in dance unite.
Brushstrokes of blue, and golden ray,
In harmony, they sway and play.

Clouds drift softly, like thoughts serene,
Reflecting dreams in shades of green.
The sun dips low, a fiery spark,
Illuminating paths through the dark.

In twilight's hush, the waters gleam,
As visions pulse, like vibrant dreams.
Every wave a note, a sweet refrain,
Singing tales of joy and pain.

With every gust, the journey calls,
In this fantasia, the spirit enthralls.
So sail into the painted skies,
Where the horizon whispers, and adventure lies.

Harmonies of the Skybound Journey

Reach for the sky, let transition start,
Each breeze a note, a dancing heart.
Where clouds compose a timeless tune,
In harmony beneath the moon.

Voyage on winds that gently sway,
Through realms of light and shades of gray.
Each feathered flight, a story spun,
Beneath the watchful, golden sun.

Celestial spheres draw us near,
With melodies we long to hear.
So follow dreams on winds that glide,
In every heartbeat, let hope reside.

So sing with joy, and leap on high,
For in this journey, we learn to fly.
With harmonies that never cease,
In skybound dreams, we find our peace.

Between Wakefulness and Slumber

In the twilight where shadows weave,
Soft whispers drift on the eve.
Thoughts linger like a gentle sigh,
As the stars begin to pry.

Eyes half-closed in muted grace,
A dance between time and space.
The mind floats on a silken thread,
In the hush where dreams are bred.

Caught between the day and night,
Fleeting visions take their flight.
Each heartbeat is a subtle call,
Echoing in the sprawling hall.

In the silence, secrets bloom,
Glimmers of a world to loom.
Between wakefulness and rest,
Lies the place where dreams are pressed.

The Poetry of Oceanic Dreams

Beneath the waves, where shadows play,
A symphony calls in the spray.
Whispers of tides in rhythmic sway,
Dance with the night, drift away.

In the depths, where wonders lie,
Creatures roam 'neath the endless sky.
Currents carve stories in sand,
Echoing love from the sea's hand.

Moonlit ripples softly gleam,
Carrying boats on a silver beam.
The ocean breathes a lullaby,
Stirring the heart with a sigh.

Beneath the surface, dreams reside,
Where secrets and magic abide.
In the depths of azure hues,
Oceanic tales inspire the muse.

The Altars of Night’s Secrets

In the cloak of the midnight air,
Ink drops fall without a care.
Beneath the stars, the shadows creep,
Guarding the secrets that they keep.

Candles flicker, the silence sings,
Hushed confessions the nighttime brings.
Each whisper wraps the moon's embrace,
Shrouded in time, a sacred space.

The cosmic dance, a ritual plain,
Where every heartbeat calls a name.
In shadows cast by ethereal light,
Lies the altar of the night.

Gathered stories, untold and bold,
In dreams of silver, in tales of gold.
A tapestry stitched with dreams so deep,
The altars where the night will weep.

A Crest of Luminous Whispers

Amidst the dawn's gentle embrace,
Luminous whispers find their place.
Soft as a feather, light as air,
A dreamy echo, a timeless prayer.

Each ray of sun, a brush of gold,
Painting secrets that gently unfold.
In the morning mist, hopes arise,
Wrapped in the warmth of sapphire skies.

Breezes carry tales of light,
Awakening hearts with pure delight.
Nature's chorus, in harmony flows,
Kissing the world as it softly glows.

With every dawn, a new refrain,
Lifting spirits, erasing pain.
In the crest where daylight gathers,
Luminous whispers are what matters.

Tales from the Ship of Dreams

In the night where whispers roam,
A ship sailed deep into the foam.
Stars danced on waves so bright,
Chasing shadows, chasing light.

Voices of the lost and found,
Echoes of a siren's sound.
With every sigh, a tale unfolds,
In the embrace of ocean's holds.

Each grain of sand, a memory spun,
Stories shared as waves outrun.
With laughter, love, and silent fears,
Time drifts softly, shedding tears.

Set your sails to dreams unknown,
In this vessel, you're not alone.
Chart a course through boundless skies,
Follow the stars where wonder lies.

Sailing Beyond the Edge of Reality

On the brink where visions blend,
Reality bows as dreams ascend.
Waves of thought surge and crash,
In a universe that spins and splashes.

Canvas skies painted with hues,
Of the truths that we can't choose.
Where echoes of laughter collide,
With fears we've chosen to confide.

Fragments of time, glimmers of light,
In the distance, the realms ignite.
Sailing forth on this endless sea,
Where every moment sets us free.

Chart the stars in heart and mind,
Leave the anchors of doubt behind.
With every tide, a new path glows,
Beyond the edge, our spirit flows.

Beneath the Starlit Mirage

Glimmers of silver in the night,
A canvas of dreams, pure delight.
Flickering shadows dance and weave,
In a place where hearts believe.

Beneath the sky's enchanting veil,
Magic finds its sacred trail.
Whispers of wishes float like dust,
In the universe, we place our trust.

Each twinkling star, a guiding light,
Navigating through the mystic night.
Here, the realms of hope ignite,
As the mirage takes its flight.

In this moment, time suspends,
Where reality and dreams amends.
Beneath the starlit gleam we stand,
Embracing wonders, hand in hand.

Fantasies on the Endless Horizon

Where the sun greets the tranquil sea,
Fantasies dance, wild and free.
Whispers ride on the salty breeze,
Carrying hopes like autumn leaves.

Every wave tells a story bold,
Of adventures waiting to unfold.
Chasing visions, we wander far,
Lit by the glow of a distant star.

Horizons stretch with tales untold,
In the warmth of dreams, we are consoled.
A canvas painted with dreams anew,
Where magic blooms in every hue.

So set your sails for the open sea,
Every heartbeat, a wild decree.
In this realm where fantasies fly,
We'll navigate 'neath the endless sky.

The Odyssey of Wishful Hearts

In dreams we sail on ships of hope,
Through waves of whispers, we learn to cope.
Our hearts like anchors, steady and true,
In the vast sea, we find our due.

With every star that guides our way,
We chase the light, come what may.
Together we wander, hand in hand,
In this odyssey, we take our stand.

The winds may shift, the storms may rise,
Yet we press on beneath the skies.
With wishful hearts, we'll light the night,
Through darkest paths, we seek the light.

For in the journey, love's the prize,
In every challenge, new hope lies.
With every heartbeat, we play our part,
This is our tale, the wishful heart.

Starlit Trails and Mystic Tides

Beneath the stars, our dreams take flight,
On mystic tides that glow so bright.
In silver shadows, we dance and sway,
Finding our balance, come what may.

The moon whispers secrets to the sea,
In twilight's arms, we long to be free.
The trails we walk beneath the night,
Guide us to worlds of pure delight.

With every wave, a story told,
Of journeys shared and hearts of gold.
We trace the paths where starlight beams,
In starlit trails, we weave our dreams.

So let the tides, like time, unfold,
With every moment, a memory bold.
In cosmic dance, our spirits rise,
In this vast space, love never dies.

Voyage of Wandering Souls

Across the seas, we search and roam,
For every heart must find its home.
In the whispers of the evening breeze,
We feel the call, we hear the pleas.

From distant shores to hidden skies,
Wandering souls seek moonlit ties.
In every step, a new-found grace,
A journey true in time and space.

With every dawn, a chance to start,
To mend the seams of a broken heart.
As waves of change begin to rise,
We hold the truth, we claim the prize.

In unity, we find our strength,
In every moment, a new length.
Together we sail, our souls ablaze,
On this voyage, through life's maze.

Chasing the Aurora's Kiss

In twilight's glow, we start our chase,
For the aurora's kiss, a fleeting grace.
With vibrant hues that dance and play,
In nature's arms, we long to stay.

The sky ignites with colors bright,
As dreams awaken in the night.
We move like shadows in the glow,
With every heartbeat, the magic flows.

Each flicker in the northern air,
Is a whisper of hope, a lover's dare.
We chase the light, we seek the thrill,
In the stillness, our spirits fill.

So take my hand, together we'll find,
The aurora's kiss, unconfined.
Through icy realms and starlit skies,
In this journey, our love will rise.

Waking Waves and Reverie

Awake from slumber’s gentle grasp,
As waves caress the golden sand,
The sun spills light, a warming clasp,
In this soft realm, dreams feel so grand.

A whisper rides on salty air,
Unfolding tales of yesteryear,
With each tide's rise, emotions bare,
Nature sings, a melody clear.

Footprints fade with the ebbing tide,
Secrets held in water’s play,
In waking waves, our hearts confide,
A reverie of night and day.

The horizon glows, a canvas bright,
Where sea and sky embrace in hue,
In waking waves, we take our flight,
And dance along the shores anew.

The Sleepwalker’s Sojourn at Sea

In twilight's hush, he roams the shore,
A sleepwalker beneath the moon,
Each step a sigh, a whispered lore,
As waves hum the sea's sweet tune.

His eyes are closed, yet visions flare,
Of ships that sail on dreams untold,
The salty breeze, a tender care,
As night unfolds its veil of gold.

He wanders deep in thought and plight,
While starlit waters beckon near,
With every dream, he takes to flight,
Exploring realms of joy and fear.

In slumber's grip, he finds the key,
Unlocking mysteries of the sea,
The sleepwalker sails, so wild and free,
Cradled in waves' eternal plea.

Mysteries Bound by Silken Tides

Deep beneath the ocean's sway,
Mysteries dance in silken veils,
Waves conceal what they betray,
As whispers ride on gentle trails.

The depths hold tales of long-lost dreams,
Where sirens sing and shadows wane,
In water's grip, time softly gleams,
Eternal secrets weave through pain.

Bound by tides, both fierce and kind,
The stories twist through night and day,
With every surge, new wonders find,
A symphony of lost array.

Mysteries bound, yet set to roam,
As currents pull and beckon near,
In silken tides, they call us home,
To dance upon the edge of fear.

A Lantern's Glow on Serene Waters

A lantern glows on waters still,
Its light a guide through misty night,
Reflecting dreams that hearts can fill,
With hope that whispers, soft and bright.

The gentle ripples kiss the shore,
As stars above begin to twinkle,
In quietude, our spirits soar,
While shadows play and night does sprinkle.

With every glow, a story wakes,
Of sailors lost and lovers found,
On serene waters, life it makes,
As time unravels, love profound.

The lantern's warmth will light the way,
Through every storm that life can weave,
On tranquil tides, we dare to stay,
In peace we find what hearts believe.

Ephemeral Horizons at Dawn

The sky blushes softly, light spills wide,
Whispers of morning, the night must hide.
Gentle hues mingle, dreams fade away,
A fleeting embrace of a new born day.

Birds take to flight, their songs afloat,
Chasing the shadows, they freely emote.
Beneath the vast canvas, hope paints the scene,
Awakening hearts to the promise serene.

Clouds drift like wishes in soft, tender grace,
Dancing the dawn in a delicate pace.
Moments are precious, let them not flee,
For time is a treasure, wild and free.

With each passing second, we gather the light,
A symphony played, the day welcomes bright.
Ephemeral visions in morning’s embrace,
Captured in silence, in time's gentle space.

Castaway Reflections on the Water

Glimmers of sunlight dance on the tide,
Whispers of secrets the waters confide.
Floating alone on a vessel of dreams,
Life's ebbs and flows, like soft silken streams.

Waves cradle memories that beckon the lost,
Adrift in the currents, we ponder the cost.
Each ripple a thought, each splash a sigh,
Where hopes intertwine and fears learn to fly.

Reflections of moments that flicker and fade,
Shadows of loves in the twilight cascade.
The heart of the ocean holds stories untold,
In whispers of water, both silent and bold.

As night draws its curtain, the stars softly gleam,
In the stillness, we find the echoes of dreams.
Castaway souls on a pilgrimage deep,
Collecting the fragments of joy while we sleep.

Whispers of a Starlit Journey

Under a canopy vast and profound,
The cosmos sings softly, a mystical sound.
With each twinkle, secrets the night will share,
Reminders of wonders that float in the air.

Footsteps in starlight, we wander the path,
Chasing the shadows, escaping the wrath.
Moments unfold like the wings of a dove,
Guided by dreams and the light of our love.

The universe beckons with stories to tell,
Enigmas of heartbeats, we journey so well.
Through echoes of laughter, through whispers of grace,
We find our reflections in vast, darkened space.

In the embrace of the night, we find our reprieve,
To dance with the stars, to hope and believe.
With each fleeting moment, our souls intertwine,
In the whispers of starlight, forever we shine.

Horizons Beyond Sleep

The night holds its breath as dreams take their flight,
Beyond every somber and silvery light.
Horizons awaken with soft lullabies,
Painting the world in magnificent skies.

Cradled in shadows, the heart learns to soar,
Unraveling mysteries that linger and pour.
In depths of the quiet, we flirt with our fears,
Reaching for memories, washing with tears.

Awake in the stillness, the silence ignites,
The promise of dawn, the end of the nights.
Horizons are stretching, horizons are vast,
Connecting the moments, the future with past.

Drifting through realms where the stars share their glow,
Learning from whispers that only we know.
With dreams as our compass, we boldly seek,
The horizons beyond, in the calm of the week.

Sailing Through Phantasmal Seas

A vessel glides on misty waves,
Ghostly whispers fill the air.
Dreams entwined with ocean's grace,
Guided by a starlit glare.

Silent tides of silver light,
Lure the hearts of those who roam.
Sailing through the endless night,
Searching for a distant home.

With each crest, a tale unfolds,
Of mariners both brave and true.
Phantasms in the deep, they mold,
A world bathed in endless blue.

Though shadows dance on foamy crests,
The horizon beams with hope.
Through every storm, the soul finds rest,
As dreams and waves together cope.

Passing Clouds and Dreaming Skies

Cotton clouds on azure trails,
Floating dreams in twilight hues.
Wandering where the heart exhales,
In the light of morning's views.

Whispers of the gentle breeze,
Carrying the laughter high.
Every moment, time's sweet tease,
Painting stories in the sky.

As sunset casts its golden glow,
Shadows dance on fields of peace.
In the twilight, thoughts will flow,
Where doubts and worries find release.

Through the night, a canvas bright,
Stars like lanterns twinkle free.
Passing clouds in peaceful flight,
Guide the heart—let dreams just be.

The Siren's Call of Pastel Horizons

In twilight’s hush, the colors blend,
Pastel whispers lure the mind.
Where dreams and reality extend,
A siren's song, so sweet, designed.

With every note, the heartstrings sway,
Ethereal visions beckon near.
On the shores where shadows play,
The gentle waves dissolve all fear.

Unraveled tides of twilight’s hue,
Hold stories of the world's embrace.
In every shade, something new,
A dance of light in endless space.

The siren's call, a tender lure,
Draws wanderers to realms untold.
In pastel dreams, the heart feels pure,
As evening's miracles unfold.

Starlit Paths of Slumber

Underneath the quilt of night,
Stars guide us through the shadows' play.
Softly glimmers, pure delight,
Leading dreams along their way.

Each twinkle tells a story rare,
Of journeys taken far and wide.
Whispers float in gentle air,
As sleep becomes a wave we ride.

In starlit paths where wishes weave,
The heart finds solace and release.
With every breath, the soul shall cleave,
To realms of magic, peace, and peace.

So close your eyes, embrace the night,
Let dreams take flight, and drift away.
Through starlit paths, we find our light,
Guided by the dawn of day.

In Search of the Dreamweaver's Port

Upon the waves of whispered song,
I seek the place where dreams belong.
A glimmering shore, where wishes bloom,
In shadows cast by twilight's gloom.

With lanterns lit in hearts anew,
I follow tides, both brave and true.
The starry map unfolds my quest,
For in this port, my soul finds rest.

The sea holds secrets in its sway,
I yearn for light to guide my way.
Through winds that dance and foam that's bright,
I chase the dawn, I seek the light.

So may I find, in tempest's roar,
The Dreamweaver's magic on the shore.
With every wave, a voice will call,
To weave my fate beneath the pall.

The Enchanted Passage

In the woods where whispers dwell,
A hidden path leads stories to tell.
Where light meets shade in playful dance,
I wander forth, lost in romance.

The trees embrace with arms so wide,
Each step reveals what hearts can hide.
In rustling leaves, I hear the lore,
Of ancient myths and tales of yore.

Through colors bright and shadows deep,
The passage weaves dreams while I sleep.
A journey brimming with secrets untold,
In every turn, a world to behold.

Oh, take my hand, sweet passage fair,
Together we'll breathe enchanted air.
Through whispers low and laughter loud,
I'll dance with you, lost in the crowd.

Currents of Imagination

In the river of thought, ideas flow,
Where dreams take flight on winds that blow.
Each ripple sparkles with bright insight,
Awakening visions in the night.

Crafted by waves of endless thought,
Imagination weaves what life forgot.
The currents shift, like time's embrace,
Inviting us to join the chase.

Across the stream of what could be,
New worlds emerge, wild and free.
With every surge, new stories rise,
Unraveled threads beneath the skies.

Let's sail this river, hand in hand,
Through the waters of our dreamland.
For in this flow, there's magic true,
Currents of hope, forever anew.

Celestial Boundaries Beneath the Stars

Under the vast celestial dome,
We wander far, we find our home.
The stars align to light our way,
As night whispers secrets to the day.

In the silence of the universe wide,
Limitless wonders, we cannot hide.
Galaxies shimmer, stories collide,
In cosmic depths, our dreams reside.

Through meteors' trails and comets' flight,
We transcend this earthly night.
Each twinkle holds a promise bright,
Of boundaries crossed, of pure delight.

So let us soar 'neath this celestial sea,
For in the stars, we truly are free.
Together we'll dance on cosmic sands,
Beyond the limits, where magic stands.

Comets and Compass Roses

In the sky where comets glide,
A compass rose waits, open wide.
Stars whisper secrets as they pass,
Guiding lost dreams with a gentle clasp.

Charting paths through twilight's glow,
Winds of change begin to blow.
Each journey maps a brand new start,
Drawing the wanderers' restless hearts.

Beneath vast skies, we find our way,
With every dawn, a new ballet.
Seas of wonder, lands untold,
In the dance of light, we are bold.

So let the comets light your path,
And compass roses show their math.
For in the night, with dreams in sight,
We sail to find our deepest flight.

Secrets of the Windborn Sail

Whispers carried on the breeze,
Secrets mingled with the seas.
The windborn sail, it knows the way,
Where shadows dance and the light may play.

Trim the sails and feel the thrill,
A path through waves, a heart to fill.
With every gust, adventure calls,
As ocean’s breath in twilight falls.

Stars above in silent keep,
Guard the dreams that we all seek.
With every swell, the stories weave,
A tapestry of those who believe.

So let the wind be your ally true,
Charting courses, both old and new.
For in the dance with ocean's grace,
We find our courage and our place.

The Restless Sea of Night Thoughts

In the stillness, shadows creep,
The restless sea, it's awake, not asleep.
Waves of thought crash on the shore,
Echoes of dreams we can't ignore.

Moonlit waters gently sigh,
Whispers of where memories lie.
Each ripple tells a tale untold,
Of passions, fears, and futures bold.

As stars reflect on liquid skin,
A beckoning call from deep within.
The sea of night, it churns and spins,
A voyage of self, where hope begins.

So let us sail on waves of thought,
For every lesson bravely fought.
In this restless sea, we dive deep,
And find the truths that we shall keep.

Drift into the Unknown

In the silence, dare to stray,
Drifting gently, come what may.
The shores behind us fade from sight,
As we embrace the coming night.

With open hearts and empty hands,
We journey far to new lands.
Each wave that breaks, a fresh new start,
Releasing burdens from the heart.

The unknown calls like a distant star,
Promising wonders from afar.
In every curl, a chance to grow,
As tides of fate begin to flow.

So let us drift, let go, and fly,
With every breath, we'll learn to try.
Into the unknown, we set our sails,
For in that voyage, no spirit fails.

A Voyage on the Wings of Night

In shadows deep, where dreams take flight,
The stars above shine silver bright.
A whisper calls from realms unknown,
Where secrets dark and wonders grown.

Across the waves of midnight's flow,
The moonlit path begins to glow.
With every gust of gentle breeze,
We sail on hopes, our hearts at ease.

Through starlit skies, we dance and glide,
On wings of night, we take our ride.
To distant lands, where magic sways,
In tranquil nights, our dreams ablaze.

In every moment, lost, yet found,
Adventure calls, it knows no bound.
As we embark, both bold and free,
A voyage blessed, just you and me.

Mysteries of the Luminous Sea

Beneath the waves, the stories hide,
In depths of blue, where shadows bide.
Glowing softly, the creatures dance,
Inviting us to take a chance.

The shimmering tides, they weave and swirl,
In twilight's grace, the secrets unfurl.
With every splash, a tale unfolds,
Of ancient dreams and treasures bold.

A realm where light meets depths of dark,
Nature's canvas, a beckoning spark.
In harmony, the currents play,
Guiding hearts in a mystical sway.

Through waves of light, we find our way,
In mysteries of night and day.
Together we dive, and together we see,
The wonders of the luminous sea.

Charting the Dreamer's Map

In lands of thought where visions grow,
A map is drawn, with care and glow.
Each line a path to what could be,
In every heart, a dreamer's plea.

The compass spins with hope's embrace,
Directing souls to their own space.
Across the stars, we travel wide,
With courage strong, and dreams as guide.

In skies adorned with colors bright,
We chart our course, igniting light.
With every step, the journey calls,
Through valleys low and mountain walls.

Through every turn, we learn and grow,
In the dreamer's realm, love's soft glow.
The map unfolds, our spirits free,
Together we journey, you and me.

The Enchanted Ship of Surreal Seas

Upon the waves, a ship does sail,
With dreams afloat, that never pale.
Its sails are spun from stardust bright,
Navigating through the veils of night.

The crew composed of whimsical dreams,
In laughter's echo, their joy redeems.
Through waters deep, where wonders gleam,
On enchanted tides, we drift and dream.

In every wave, a tale awaits,
Of distant lands and change of fates.
With every gust, the magic grows,
As we embrace what the ocean knows.

The ship shall guide through realms unseen,
Awash with colors rich and keen.
Together we sail, both brave and free,
On the enchanted ship of surreal seas.

Moonlit Waters

Beneath the moon's soft gaze, they glow,
Ripples dance in silvered flow,
Stars twinkle in the velvet night,
Guiding dreams to take their flight.

Whispers ride the evening breeze,
Secrets shared among the trees,
A serenade of tranquil sound,
In this haven, peace is found.

Reflections shimmer on the tide,
Nature's canvas stretched wide,
Echoes of a distant tune,
Cradled by the light of moon.

In twilight's charm, our spirits sway,
As time drifts lazily away,
Lost in thought, we gently roam,
These moonlit waters feel like home.

Whispered Secrets

In shadows deep where silence lives,
Hidden tales the night now gives,
Echoes soft, like stolen glances,
Invite us to embrace our chances.

A breeze that carries distant sighs,
Entwined with dreams, it softly flies,
Through ancient woods where secrets twine,
In every leaf, a story's line.

Lovers' vows under a starry cloak,
Voices merge, a tender stroke,
With every glance, a promise made,
In whispered tones, fears will fade.

As dawn approaches, truths emerge,
Illuminated by the surge,
Of warmth that sweeps the dark away,
And births a bright, new day.

Celestial Trails of Imagination

Across the skies, where dreams ignite,
Celestial trails paint the night,
With colors brushed by starlit hands,
Infinite realms where wonder stands.

Comets blaze and galaxies swirl,
In the heart of a twinkling pearl,
Each spark a whisper from the past,
In cosmic tales that forever last.

Boundless thoughts take flight anew,
In every hue, a chance to view,
The mysteries of the universe wide,
In imagination, we will glide.

So let us soar beyond the stars,
Chasing dreams, forgetting scars,
For in this vast and endless scheme,
Life's but a canvas, bold with dream.

The Uncharted Waters of Reverie

Among the waves of thought untamed,
In uncharted waters, dreams are framed,
Each swell a notion yet to find,
In realms where hearts and hopes unwind.

With gentle hands, the sea will guide,
As visions rise upon the tide,
Sailing through the misty dawn,
We chase the shadows, swiftly drawn.

A tapestry of wishes weave,
In sight of shores we dare believe,
Drifting on the currents fine,
In reverie, our souls design.

Embrace the depth, the unknown sway,
For in this journey, we must stay,
Unlocking treasures meant to shine,
In waters deep, eternal, divine.

Fantasia on the Ocean's Breath

The ocean breathes a timeless song,
Where waves and dreams both belong,
With every crest, a tale unfolds,
In whispers soft, the sea retolds.

With salty air and sunlit gleams,
The surf enchants with liquid dreams,
Dancing shells and foamy spray,
Invite us to the depths of play.

As tides embrace the golden shore,
We find our hearts forevermore,
In melodies of ebb and flow,
Together, let our spirits grow.

So join the waltz of nature's grace,
Where time and tides embrace,
In fantasia, we'll drift and roam,
For on the ocean's breath, we're home.

The Navigator of Night’s Whims

Underneath the silver glow,
A ship sails where shadows flow.
With whispered winds, the stars align,
In dreams, the midnight lanterns shine.

Through tides of visions, vast and deep,
In twilight's embrace, our secrets keep.
The moonlight's map guides each desire,
In cosmic dances, hearts conspire.

With every wave, a story's told,
In the dark, our spirits bold.
An endless journey, a serenade,
On oceans where our fears can fade.

Together, we chase the fleeting light,
As hope ignites the endless night.
Through realms unseen, our spirits roam,
In night's vast arms, we find our home.

Oceans of Unraveled Fantasies

Waves of dreams upon the shore,
Whispers echo, then restore.
Currents pull with gentle ease,
In depths of thought, we are at peace.

Sailing forth on thought's vast sea,
Every crest holds mystery.
Castles built from fleeting bliss,
In the sun's warm, golden kiss.

The horizon's edge, a painted hue,
Guides us toward the vast anew.
With every breath, we dive and play,
In the ocean's arms, we drift away.

The tides recede, the moon is high,
Under starlit dreams, we fly.
Together, we sketch endless sights,
On the canvas of endless nights.

When Stars Become Our Compass

In the quiet of the night,
Stars above shine pure and bright.
To navigate through fears and doubts,
In cosmos' glow, the heart shouts.

With each flicker, dreams ignite,
Guiding souls through darkened flight.
Galaxies whisper, secrets shared,
With constellations, we are paired.

Across the sky, we trace our path,
In celestial dance, we find our math.
The universe unfolds its plan,
Uniting woman, child, and man.

When shadows loom, we'll stand as one,
Beneath the same enchanted sun.
Together we wander, hand in hand,
With starry eyes, forever we stand.

Wandering through the Veil of Dreams

In a world where silence sings,
We seek the joy that dreaming brings.
Through veils of night, illusions play,
In whispered thoughts, we lose our way.

Clouds of hope drift soft and light,
Painting visions through the night.
Each step forward, a new surprise,
Where wonder glimmers in our eyes.

In fields of thought, we dance and twirl,
Through secret paths, our stories unfurl.
With every breath, the magic sways,
Illuminating countless pathways.

Through soft shadows, we explore,
Finding treasures on dreams' vast shore.
Together, we mold the twilight's seam,
Endlessly wandering through the dream.

The Celestial Navigator’s Tale

In the stillness of the night,
Stars whisper secrets, shining bright.
Guiding hands on the helm,
In the vastness, I find my realm.

Waves of silver dance and play,
Charting courses, come what may.
The moon's glow a faithful guide,
In this journey, I abide.

Constellations spell my name,
Each twinkle, a spark of flame.
With every breath, the cosmos sings,
To the heart of a sailor, it brings.

Through dark skies, I navigate,
Finding peace in the stellar fate.
A tale woven in cosmic thread,
As I follow where the stars have led.

Reflections on the Waters of Night

Silvery ripples break the glass,
Soft whispers of the night have passed.
Moonlight dances on the stream,
In its glow, I find my dream.

Beneath the surface, secrets hide,
In the depths, where shadows bide.
Glimmers of hope, shining bright,
In the stillness of the night.

Feathers of clouds gently drift,
Carrying the heart's own gift.
Reflections echo stories told,
In the waters, dreams unfold.

As the stars alight above,
They twinkle like the eyes of love.
In night's embrace, I find my place,
With every wave, a soft trace.

Boundless Journeys through Mind's Ocean

In the chamber of my soul,
Thoughts like waves begin to roll.
Navigating through the deep,
Where memories and visions seep.

Currents pull me to the past,
Echoes of moments fading fast.
Imagination sets me free,
In the ocean, I find me.

Dreams unfurl like sails in wind,
Boundless horizons twist and bend.
With each thought, a journey starts,
Through the waters of our hearts.

Drifting far, yet anchored near,
In this ocean, I persevere.
With waves of wisdom, I do glide,
Across the mind's vast, endless tide.

Celestial Currents and Wind's Embrace

Breezes whisper secrets soft,
Through the leaves, they swirl aloft.
In the twilight's soothing grace,
I find peace in nature's face.

Stars ignite the evening's dome,
Guiding wanderers safely home.
Celestial currents beckon me,
On air's wings, I yearn to be.

The wind carries tales untold,
In its breath, adventures bold.
It kisses the earth with delight,
In every gust, a spark of light.

As I wander through the vast,
Each moment cherished, none too fast.
With open arms, I chase the breeze,
In the dance of life, I find my ease.

Milton Keynes UK
Ingram Content Group UK Ltd.
UKHW020735301124
451807UK00019B/789

9 789916 90765